YOUR DREAMS
ARE ONLY
Dreams
UNTIL YOU
WRITE THEM DOWN...
THEN THEY ARE
Goals

This Journal Belongs to

HOW TO USE THIS BOOK

AND MAKE SURE YOU ACTUALLY STICK TO YOUR RESOLUTIONS AND ACHIEVE YOUR GOALS

You didn't achieve your New Year's resolutions last year. I say that instead of asking it because I'm confident it's probably true. According to Forbes, only 8% of people achieve their New Year's resolutions.

Now, how do you get into that 8%? Well, looks like you're already on the right track because you took the initiative and got this goal crushing journal. The next step is using this journal effectively and pairing it with action.

Think of this as your toolbox. We've constructed this journal to give you everything you need to succeed. All you have to do is the work. You have the road map. Now you just need to start the engine and step on the gas. I think that's enough analogies, but you get it. Just like you're going to get to the end of the year and pat yourself on the back because you made it into that 8%.

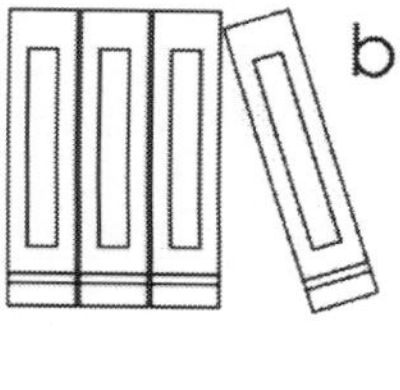

Be specific: When you're setting your goals, get as detailed as possible. For example, instead of saying "I'm going to be healthy this year," say "I'm going to go running three times a week."

Be realistic: Make sure they are achievable. Research shows that people are most successful in achieving their goals when they break them down into small milestones. Those who set lofty goals that are far out of reach usually end up getting frustrated and giving up. For example, if it takes you 10 minutes to run a mile and you want to run it in 5, you wouldn't make 5 minutes your goal. You would start by making your goal 9 minutes, 8 minute and then slowly work your way to 5.

Measure progress: "If you can't measure it, you can't change it." - Peter Drucker
Being able to measure your progress will motivate you and help you adjust your behavior to stay on track. If you see you're doing great, pat yourself on the back. If you see you're slipping backwards, step up your game.

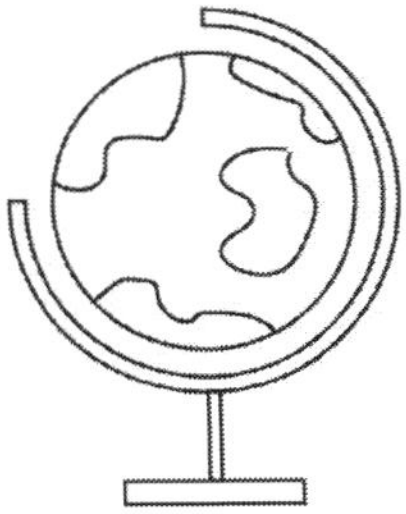

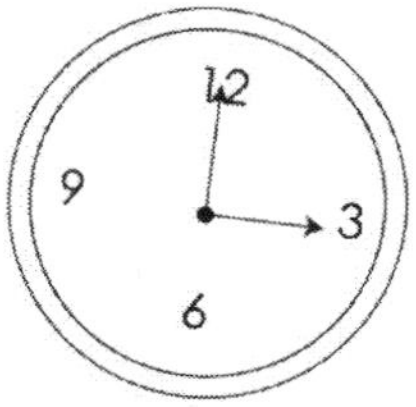

Schedule time:
"The key is not to prioritize what's on your schedule, but to schedule your priorities." - Stephen Covey We're all busy, so it is up to us to make time for the things that matter. Grab your planner or calendar and set a time for when you are going to do the work.

It's not all or nothing: This isn't the "go hard or go home" mentality. When it comes to achieving your goals, any effort towards your goal is better than no effort at all. So say you don't have the energy to run a whole mile. Instead of skipping and waiting until tomorrow, run a half mile instead.

Find accountability:It's easy to make and break promises to yourself, but it's a lot tougher to do that with someone else. Tell a friend, family member, or someone else on the internet like an accountability partner (yes, there's forums for everything) your goal and weekly progress. Be courageous and do this because it will dramatically boost your odds of success.

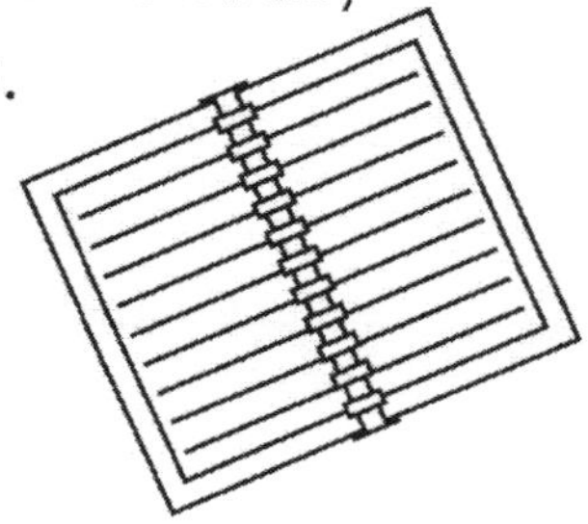

GOALS

I CAN DO THIS

I AM GOING TO

ACTION/PLAN

ACTION STEPS & MILESTONES
☐
☐
☐
☐
☐
☐
☐
☐
☐
☐
☐
☐
☐
☐

- [ ]
- [ ]
- [ ]
- [ ]
- [ ]
- [ ]
- [ ]
- [ ]
- [ ]
- [ ]
- [ ]
- [ ]
- [ ]
- [ ]
- [ ]
- [ ]
- [ ]

ACCOUNTABILITY/ PARTNER	SCHEDULE	DAY	TIME

GOALS

I CAN DO THIS

I AM GOING TO

ACTION/PLAN

ACTION STEPS & MILESTONES
☐
☐
☐
☐
☐
☐
☐
☐
☐
☐
☐
☐
☐
☐

ACCOUNTABILITY/ PARTNER	SCHEDULE	DAY	TIME

GOALS

I CAN DO THIS

I AM GOING TO

ACTION/PLAN

ACTION STEPS & MILESTONES
☐
☐
☐
☐
☐
☐
☐
☐
☐
☐
☐
☐
☐
☐

- [ ]
- [ ]
- [ ]
- [ ]
- [ ]
- [ ]
- [ ]
- [ ]
- [ ]
- [ ]
- [ ]
- [ ]
- [ ]
- [ ]
- [ ]
- [ ]
- [ ]

ACCOUNTABILITY/ PARTNER	SCHEDULE	DAY	TIME

GOALS

I CAN DO THIS

I AM GOING TO

ACTION/PLAN

ACTION STEPS & MILESTONES
☐
☐
☐
☐
☐
☐
☐
☐
☐
☐
☐
☐
☐
☐

- [ ]
- [ ]
- [ ]
- [ ]
- [ ]
- [ ]
- [ ]
- [ ]
- [ ]
- [ ]
- [ ]
- [ ]
- [ ]
- [ ]
- [ ]
- [ ]
- [ ]

ACCOUNTABILITY/ PARTNER	SCHEDULE	DAY	TIME

GOALS

I CAN DO THIS

I AM GOING TO

ACTION/PLAN

ACTION STEPS & MILESTONES
☐
☐
☐
☐
☐
☐
☐
☐
☐
☐
☐
☐
☐
☐

- [ ]
- [ ]
- [ ]
- [ ]
- [ ]
- [ ]
- [ ]
- [ ]
- [ ]
- [ ]
- [ ]
- [ ]
- [ ]
- [ ]
- [ ]
- [ ]
- [ ]

ACCOUNTABILITY/ PARTNER	SCHEDULE	DAY	TIME

GOALS

I CAN DO THIS

I AM GOING TO

ACTION/PLAN

ACTION STEPS & MILESTONES
☐
☐
☐
☐
☐
☐
☐
☐
☐
☐
☐
☐
☐
☐

- [ ]
- [ ]
- [ ]
- [ ]
- [ ]
- [ ]
- [ ]
- [ ]
- [ ]
- [ ]
- [ ]
- [ ]
- [ ]
- [ ]
- [ ]
- [ ]
- [ ]

ACCOUNTABILITY/ PARTNER	SCHEDULE	DAY	TIME

GOALS

I CAN DO THIS

I AM GOING TO

ACTION/PLAN

ACTION STEPS & MILESTONES
☐
☐
☐
☐
☐
☐
☐
☐
☐
☐
☐
☐
☐
☐

☐
☐
☐
☐
☐
☐
☐
☐
☐
☐
☐
☐
☐
☐
☐
☐
☐

ACCOUNTABILITY/ PARTNER	SCHEDULE	DAY	TIME

GOALS

I CAN DO THIS

I AM GOING TO

ACTION/PLAN

ACTION STEPS & MILESTONES
☐
☐
☐
☐
☐
☐
☐
☐
☐
☐
☐
☐
☐
☐

☐
☐
☐
☐
☐
☐
☐
☐
☐
☐
☐
☐
☐
☐
☐
☐
☐

ACCOUNTABILITY/ PARTNER	SCHEDULE	DAY	TIME

GOALS

I CAN DO THIS

I AM GOING TO

ACTION/PLAN

ACTION STEPS & MILESTONES

- ☐
- ☐
- ☐
- ☐
- ☐
- ☐
- ☐
- ☐
- ☐
- ☐
- ☐
- ☐
- ☐
- ☐

- [ ]
- [ ]
- [ ]
- [ ]
- [ ]
- [ ]
- [ ]
- [ ]
- [ ]
- [ ]
- [ ]
- [ ]
- [ ]
- [ ]
- [ ]
- [ ]
- [ ]

ACCOUNTABILITY/ PARTNER	SCHEDULE	DAY	TIME

GOALS

I CAN DO THIS

I AM GOING TO

ACTION/PLAN

ACTION STEPS & MILESTONES
☐
☐
☐
☐
☐
☐
☐
☐
☐
☐
☐
☐
☐
☐

☐
☐
☐
☐
☐
☐
☐
☐
☐
☐
☐
☐
☐
☐
☐
☐
☐

ACCOUNTABILITY/ PARTNER	SCHEDULE	DAY	TIME

GOALS

I CAN DO THIS

I AM GOING TO

ACTION/PLAN

ACTION STEPS & MILESTONES
☐
☐
☐
☐
☐
☐
☐
☐
☐
☐
☐
☐
☐
☐

☐
☐
☐
☐
☐
☐
☐
☐
☐
☐
☐
☐
☐
☐
☐
☐
☐

ACCOUNTABILITY/ PARTNER	SCHEDULE	DAY	TIME

GOALS

I CAN DO THIS

I AM GOING TO

ACTION/PLAN

ACTION STEPS & MILESTONES
☐
☐
☐
☐
☐
☐
☐
☐
☐
☐
☐
☐
☐
☐

- [ ]
- [ ]
- [ ]
- [ ]
- [ ]
- [ ]
- [ ]
- [ ]
- [ ]
- [ ]
- [ ]
- [ ]
- [ ]
- [ ]
- [ ]
- [ ]
- [ ]

ACCOUNTABILITY/ PARTNER	SCHEDULE	DAY	TIME

GOALS

I CAN DO THIS

I AM GOING TO

ACTION/PLAN

ACTION STEPS & MILESTONES
☐
☐
☐
☐
☐
☐
☐
☐
☐
☐
☐
☐
☐
☐

- [ ]
- [ ]
- [ ]
- [ ]
- [ ]
- [ ]
- [ ]
- [ ]
- [ ]
- [ ]
- [ ]
- [ ]
- [ ]
- [ ]
- [ ]
- [ ]
- [ ]

ACCOUNTABILITY/ PARTNER	SCHEDULE	DAY	TIME

GOALS

I CAN DO THIS

I AM GOING TO

ACTION/PLAN

ACTION STEPS & MILESTONES

- [ ]
- [ ]
- [ ]
- [ ]
- [ ]
- [ ]
- [ ]
- [ ]
- [ ]
- [ ]
- [ ]
- [ ]
- [ ]
- [ ]

- [ ]
- [ ]
- [ ]
- [ ]
- [ ]
- [ ]
- [ ]
- [ ]
- [ ]
- [ ]
- [ ]
- [ ]
- [ ]
- [ ]
- [ ]
- [ ]
- [ ]

ACCOUNTABILITY/ PARTNER	SCHEDULE	DAY	TIME

GOALS

I CAN DO THIS

I AM GOING TO

ACTION/PLAN

ACTION STEPS & MILESTONES
☐
☐
☐
☐
☐
☐
☐
☐
☐
☐
☐
☐
☐
☐

- [ ]
- [ ]
- [ ]
- [ ]
- [ ]
- [ ]
- [ ]
- [ ]
- [ ]
- [ ]
- [ ]
- [ ]
- [ ]
- [ ]
- [ ]
- [ ]
- [ ]

ACCOUNTABILITY/ PARTNER	SCHEDULE	DAY	TIME

GOALS

I CAN DO THIS

I AM GOING TO

ACTION/PLAN

ACTION STEPS & MILESTONES
☐
☐
☐
☐
☐
☐
☐
☐
☐
☐
☐
☐
☐
☐

- [ ]
- [ ]
- [ ]
- [ ]
- [ ]
- [ ]
- [ ]
- [ ]
- [ ]
- [ ]
- [ ]
- [ ]
- [ ]
- [ ]
- [ ]
- [ ]
- [ ]

ACCOUNTABILITY/ PARTNER	SCHEDULE	DAY	TIME

GOALS

I CAN DO THIS

I AM GOING TO

ACTION/PLAN

ACTION STEPS & MILESTONES
☐
☐
☐
☐
☐
☐
☐
☐
☐
☐
☐
☐
☐
☐

- [ ]
- [ ]
- [ ]
- [ ]
- [ ]
- [ ]
- [ ]
- [ ]
- [ ]
- [ ]
- [ ]
- [ ]
- [ ]
- [ ]
- [ ]
- [ ]
- [ ]

ACCOUNTABILITY/ PARTNER	SCHEDULE	DAY	TIME

GOALS

I CAN DO THIS

I AM GOING TO

ACTION/PLAN

ACTION STEPS & MILESTONES
☐
☐
☐
☐
☐
☐
☐
☐
☐
☐
☐
☐
☐
☐

☐
☐
☐
☐
☐
☐
☐
☐
☐
☐
☐
☐
☐
☐
☐
☐
☐

ACCOUNTABILITY/ PARTNER	SCHEDULE	DAY	TIME

GOALS

I CAN DO THIS

I AM GOING TO

ACTION/PLAN

ACTION STEPS & MILESTONES
☐
☐
☐
☐
☐
☐
☐
☐
☐
☐
☐
☐
☐
☐

ACCOUNTABILITY/ PARTNER	SCHEDULE	DAY	TIME

GOALS

I CAN DO THIS

I AM GOING TO

ACTION/PLAN

ACTION STEPS & MILESTONES
☐
☐
☐
☐
☐
☐
☐
☐
☐
☐
☐
☐
☐
☐

- [ ]
- [ ]
- [ ]
- [ ]
- [ ]
- [ ]
- [ ]
- [ ]
- [ ]
- [ ]
- [ ]
- [ ]
- [ ]
- [ ]
- [ ]
- [ ]
- [ ]

ACCOUNTABILITY/ PARTNER	SCHEDULE	DAY	TIME

GOALS

I CAN DO THIS

I AM GOING TO

ACTION/PLAN

ACTION STEPS & MILESTONES
☐
☐
☐
☐
☐
☐
☐
☐
☐
☐
☐
☐
☐
☐

ACCOUNTABILITY/ PARTNER	SCHEDULE	DAY	TIME

GOALS

I CAN DO THIS

I AM GOING TO

ACTION/PLAN

ACTION STEPS & MILESTONES
☐
☐
☐
☐
☐
☐
☐
☐
☐
☐
☐
☐
☐
☐

- [ ]
- [ ]
- [ ]
- [ ]
- [ ]
- [ ]
- [ ]
- [ ]
- [ ]
- [ ]
- [ ]
- [ ]
- [ ]
- [ ]
- [ ]
- [ ]
- [ ]

ACCOUNTABILITY/ PARTNER	SCHEDULE	DAY	TIME

GOALS

I CAN DO THIS

I AM GOING TO

ACTION/PLAN

ACTION STEPS & MILESTONES
☐
☐
☐
☐
☐
☐
☐
☐
☐
☐
☐
☐
☐
☐

- [ ]
- [ ]
- [ ]
- [ ]
- [ ]
- [ ]
- [ ]
- [ ]
- [ ]
- [ ]
- [ ]
- [ ]
- [ ]
- [ ]
- [ ]
- [ ]
- [ ]

ACCOUNTABILITY/ PARTNER	SCHEDULE	DAY	TIME

GOALS

I CAN DO THIS

I AM GOING TO

ACTION/PLAN

ACTION STEPS & MILESTONES
☐
☐
☐
☐
☐
☐
☐
☐
☐
☐
☐
☐
☐
☐

☐
☐
☐
☐
☐
☐
☐
☐
☐
☐
☐
☐
☐
☐
☐
☐
☐

ACCOUNTABILITY/ PARTNER	SCHEDULE	DAY	TIME

GOALS

I CAN DO THIS

I AM GOING TO

ACTION/PLAN

ACTION STEPS & MILESTONES
☐
☐
☐
☐
☐
☐
☐
☐
☐
☐
☐
☐
☐
☐

- [ ]
- [ ]
- [ ]
- [ ]
- [ ]
- [ ]
- [ ]
- [ ]
- [ ]
- [ ]
- [ ]
- [ ]
- [ ]
- [ ]
- [ ]
- [ ]
- [ ]

ACCOUNTABILITY/ PARTNER	SCHEDULE	DAY	TIME

GOALS

I CAN DO THIS

I AM GOING TO

ACTION/PLAN

ACTION STEPS & MILESTONES
☐
☐
☐
☐
☐
☐
☐
☐
☐
☐
☐
☐
☐
☐

- [ ]
- [ ]
- [ ]
- [ ]
- [ ]
- [ ]
- [ ]
- [ ]
- [ ]
- [ ]
- [ ]
- [ ]
- [ ]
- [ ]
- [ ]
- [ ]
- [ ]

ACCOUNTABILITY/ PARTNER	SCHEDULE	DAY	TIME

GOALS

I CAN DO THIS

I AM GOING TO

ACTION/PLAN

ACTION STEPS & MILESTONES
☐
☐
☐
☐
☐
☐
☐
☐
☐
☐
☐
☐
☐
☐

- [ ]
- [ ]
- [ ]
- [ ]
- [ ]
- [ ]
- [ ]
- [ ]
- [ ]
- [ ]
- [ ]
- [ ]
- [ ]
- [ ]
- [ ]
- [ ]
- [ ]

ACCOUNTABILITY/ PARTNER	SCHEDULE	DAY	TIME

GOALS

I CAN DO THIS

I AM GOING TO

ACTION/PLAN

ACTION STEPS & MILESTONES
☐
☐
☐
☐
☐
☐
☐
☐
☐
☐
☐
☐
☐
☐

- [ ]
- [ ]
- [ ]
- [ ]
- [ ]
- [ ]
- [ ]
- [ ]
- [ ]
- [ ]
- [ ]
- [ ]
- [ ]
- [ ]
- [ ]
- [ ]
- [ ]

ACCOUNTABILITY/ PARTNER	SCHEDULE	DAY	TIME

GOALS

I CAN DO THIS

I AM GOING TO

ACTION/PLAN

ACTION STEPS & MILESTONES
☐
☐
☐
☐
☐
☐
☐
☐
☐
☐
☐
☐
☐
☐

- [ ]
- [ ]
- [ ]
- [ ]
- [ ]
- [ ]
- [ ]
- [ ]
- [ ]
- [ ]
- [ ]
- [ ]
- [ ]
- [ ]
- [ ]
- [ ]
- [ ]

ACCOUNTABILITY/ PARTNER	SCHEDULE	DAY	TIME

GOALS

I CAN DO THIS

I AM GOING TO

ACTION/PLAN

ACTION STEPS & MILESTONES
☐
☐
☐
☐
☐
☐
☐
☐
☐
☐
☐
☐
☐
☐

- [ ]
- [ ]
- [ ]
- [ ]
- [ ]
- [ ]
- [ ]
- [ ]
- [ ]
- [ ]
- [ ]
- [ ]
- [ ]
- [ ]
- [ ]
- [ ]
- [ ]

ACCOUNTABILITY/ PARTNER	SCHEDULE	DAY	TIME

GOALS

I CAN DO THIS

I AM GOING TO

ACTION/PLAN

ACTION STEPS & MILESTONES
☐
☐
☐
☐
☐
☐
☐
☐
☐
☐
☐
☐
☐
☐

- [ ]
- [ ]
- [ ]
- [ ]
- [ ]
- [ ]
- [ ]
- [ ]
- [ ]
- [ ]
- [ ]
- [ ]
- [ ]
- [ ]
- [ ]
- [ ]
- [ ]

ACCOUNTABILITY/ PARTNER	SCHEDULE	DAY	TIME

GOALS

I CAN DO THIS

I AM GOING TO

ACTION/PLAN

ACTION STEPS & MILESTONES
☐
☐
☐
☐
☐
☐
☐
☐
☐
☐
☐
☐
☐
☐

- [ ]
- [ ]
- [ ]
- [ ]
- [ ]
- [ ]
- [ ]
- [ ]
- [ ]
- [ ]
- [ ]
- [ ]
- [ ]
- [ ]
- [ ]
- [ ]
- [ ]

ACCOUNTABILITY/ PARTNER	SCHEDULE	DAY	TIME

GOALS

I CAN DO THIS

I AM GOING TO

ACTION/PLAN

ACTION STEPS & MILESTONES
☐
☐
☐
☐
☐
☐
☐
☐
☐
☐
☐
☐
☐
☐

☐
☐
☐
☐
☐
☐
☐
☐
☐
☐
☐
☐
☐
☐
☐
☐
☐

ACCOUNTABILITY/ PARTNER	SCHEDULE	DAY	TIME

GOALS

I CAN DO THIS

I AM GOING TO

ACTION/PLAN

ACTION STEPS & MILESTONES
☐
☐
☐
☐
☐
☐
☐
☐
☐
☐
☐
☐
☐
☐

☐

☐

☐

☐

☐

☐

☐

☐

☐

☐

☐

☐

☐

☐

☐

☐

☐

ACCOUNTABILITY/ PARTNER	SCHEDULE	DAY	TIME

GOALS

I CAN DO THIS

I AM GOING TO

ACTION/PLAN

ACTION STEPS & MILESTONES
☐
☐
☐
☐
☐
☐
☐
☐
☐
☐
☐
☐
☐
☐

- [ ]
- [ ]
- [ ]
- [ ]
- [ ]
- [ ]
- [ ]
- [ ]
- [ ]
- [ ]
- [ ]
- [ ]
- [ ]
- [ ]
- [ ]
- [ ]
- [ ]

ACCOUNTABILITY/ PARTNER	SCHEDULE	DAY	TIME

GOALS

I CAN DO THIS

I AM GOING TO

ACTION/PLAN

ACTION STEPS & MILESTONES
☐
☐
☐
☐
☐
☐
☐
☐
☐
☐
☐
☐
☐
☐

- [ ]
- [ ]
- [ ]
- [ ]
- [ ]
- [ ]
- [ ]
- [ ]
- [ ]
- [ ]
- [ ]
- [ ]
- [ ]
- [ ]
- [ ]
- [ ]
- [ ]

ACCOUNTABILITY/ PARTNER	SCHEDULE	DAY	TIME

GOALS

I CAN DO THIS

I AM GOING TO

ACTION/PLAN

ACTION STEPS & MILESTONES
☐
☐
☐
☐
☐
☐
☐
☐
☐
☐
☐
☐
☐
☐

- [ ]
- [ ]
- [ ]
- [ ]
- [ ]
- [ ]
- [ ]
- [ ]
- [ ]
- [ ]
- [ ]
- [ ]
- [ ]
- [ ]
- [ ]
- [ ]
- [ ]

ACCOUNTABILITY/ PARTNER	SCHEDULE	DAY	TIME

GOALS

I CAN DO THIS

I AM GOING TO

ACTION/PLAN

ACTION STEPS & MILESTONES
☐
☐
☐
☐
☐
☐
☐
☐
☐
☐
☐
☐
☐
☐

- [ ]
- [ ]
- [ ]
- [ ]
- [ ]
- [ ]
- [ ]
- [ ]
- [ ]
- [ ]
- [ ]
- [ ]
- [ ]
- [ ]
- [ ]
- [ ]
- [ ]

ACCOUNTABILITY/ PARTNER	SCHEDULE	DAY	TIME

GOALS

I CAN DO THIS

I AM GOING TO

ACTION/PLAN

ACTION STEPS & MILESTONES
☐
☐
☐
☐
☐
☐
☐
☐
☐
☐
☐
☐
☐
☐

ACCOUNTABILITY/ PARTNER	SCHEDULE	DAY	TIME

GOALS

I CAN DO THIS

I AM GOING TO

ACTION/PLAN

ACTION STEPS & MILESTONES
☐
☐
☐
☐
☐
☐
☐
☐
☐
☐
☐
☐
☐
☐

ACCOUNTABILITY/ PARTNER	SCHEDULE	DAY	TIME

GOALS

I CAN DO THIS

I AM GOING TO

ACTION/PLAN

ACTION STEPS & MILESTONES
☐
☐
☐
☐
☐
☐
☐
☐
☐
☐
☐
☐
☐
☐

ACCOUNTABILITY/ PARTNER	SCHEDULE	DAY	TIME

GOALS

I CAN DO THIS

I AM GOING TO

ACTION/PLAN

ACTION STEPS & MILESTONES
☐
☐
☐
☐
☐
☐
☐
☐
☐
☐
☐
☐
☐
☐

- [ ]
- [ ]
- [ ]
- [ ]
- [ ]
- [ ]
- [ ]
- [ ]
- [ ]
- [ ]
- [ ]
- [ ]
- [ ]
- [ ]
- [ ]
- [ ]
- [ ]

ACCOUNTABILITY/ PARTNER	SCHEDULE	DAY	TIME

GOALS

I CAN DO THIS

I AM GOING TO

ACTION/PLAN

ACTION STEPS & MILESTONES
☐
☐
☐
☐
☐
☐
☐
☐
☐
☐
☐
☐
☐
☐

- [ ]
- [ ]
- [ ]
- [ ]
- [ ]
- [ ]
- [ ]
- [ ]
- [ ]
- [ ]
- [ ]
- [ ]
- [ ]
- [ ]
- [ ]
- [ ]
- [ ]

ACCOUNTABILITY/ PARTNER	SCHEDULE	DAY	TIME

GOALS

I CAN DO THIS

I AM GOING TO

ACTION/PLAN

ACTION STEPS & MILESTONES
☐
☐
☐
☐
☐
☐
☐
☐
☐
☐
☐
☐
☐
☐

- [ ]
- [ ]
- [ ]
- [ ]
- [ ]
- [ ]
- [ ]
- [ ]
- [ ]
- [ ]
- [ ]
- [ ]
- [ ]
- [ ]
- [ ]
- [ ]
- [ ]

ACCOUNTABILITY/ PARTNER	SCHEDULE	DAY	TIME

GOALS

I CAN DO THIS

I AM GOING TO

ACTION/PLAN

ACTION STEPS & MILESTONES
☐
☐
☐
☐
☐
☐
☐
☐
☐
☐
☐
☐
☐
☐

- [ ]
- [ ]
- [ ]
- [ ]
- [ ]
- [ ]
- [ ]
- [ ]
- [ ]
- [ ]
- [ ]
- [ ]
- [ ]
- [ ]
- [ ]
- [ ]
- [ ]

ACCOUNTABILITY/ PARTNER	SCHEDULE	DAY	TIME

GOALS

I CAN DO THIS

I AM GOING TO

ACTION/PLAN

ACTION STEPS & MILESTONES
☐
☐
☐
☐
☐
☐
☐
☐
☐
☐
☐
☐
☐
☐

☐
☐
☐
☐
☐
☐
☐
☐
☐
☐
☐
☐
☐
☐
☐
☐
☐

ACCOUNTABILITY/ PARTNER	SCHEDULE	DAY	TIME

GOALS

I CAN DO THIS

I AM GOING TO

ACTION/PLAN

ACTION STEPS & MILESTONES
☐
☐
☐
☐
☐
☐
☐
☐
☐
☐
☐
☐
☐
☐

- [ ]
- [ ]
- [ ]
- [ ]
- [ ]
- [ ]
- [ ]
- [ ]
- [ ]
- [ ]
- [ ]
- [ ]
- [ ]
- [ ]
- [ ]
- [ ]
- [ ]

ACCOUNTABILITY/ PARTNER	SCHEDULE	DAY	TIME

GOALS

I CAN DO THIS

I AM GOING TO

ACTION/PLAN

ACTION STEPS & MILESTONES
☐
☐
☐
☐
☐
☐
☐
☐
☐
☐
☐
☐
☐
☐

☐
☐
☐
☐
☐
☐
☐
☐
☐
☐
☐
☐
☐
☐
☐
☐
☐

ACCOUNTABILITY/ PARTNER	SCHEDULE	DAY	TIME

GOALS

I CAN DO THIS

I AM GOING TO

ACTION/PLAN

ACTION STEPS & MILESTONES
☐
☐
☐
☐
☐
☐
☐
☐
☐
☐
☐
☐
☐
☐

☐

☐

☐

☐

☐

☐

☐

☐

☐

☐

☐

☐

☐

☐

☐

☐

☐

ACCOUNTABILITY/ PARTNER	SCHEDULE	DAY	TIME

GOALS

I CAN DO THIS

I AM GOING TO

ACTION/PLAN

ACTION STEPS & MILESTONES
☐
☐
☐
☐
☐
☐
☐
☐
☐
☐
☐
☐
☐
☐

- [ ]
- [ ]
- [ ]
- [ ]
- [ ]
- [ ]
- [ ]
- [ ]
- [ ]
- [ ]
- [ ]
- [ ]
- [ ]
- [ ]
- [ ]
- [ ]
- [ ]

ACCOUNTABILITY/ PARTNER	SCHEDULE	DAY	TIME

GOALS

I CAN DO THIS

I AM GOING TO

ACTION/PLAN

ACTION STEPS & MILESTONES
☐
☐
☐
☐
☐
☐
☐
☐
☐
☐
☐
☐
☐
☐

☐
☐
☐
☐
☐
☐
☐
☐
☐
☐
☐
☐
☐
☐
☐
☐
☐

ACCOUNTABILITY/ PARTNER	SCHEDULE	DAY	TIME

GOALS

I CAN DO THIS

I AM GOING TO

ACTION/PLAN

ACTION STEPS & MILESTONES

- [ ]
- [ ]
- [ ]
- [ ]
- [ ]
- [ ]
- [ ]
- [ ]
- [ ]
- [ ]
- [ ]
- [ ]
- [ ]
- [ ]

- [ ]
- [ ]
- [ ]
- [ ]
- [ ]
- [ ]
- [ ]
- [ ]
- [ ]
- [ ]
- [ ]
- [ ]
- [ ]
- [ ]
- [ ]
- [ ]
- [ ]

ACCOUNTABILITY/ PARTNER	SCHEDULE	DAY	TIME

GOALS

I CAN DO THIS

I AM GOING TO

ACTION/PLAN

ACTION STEPS & MILESTONES
☐
☐
☐
☐
☐
☐
☐
☐
☐
☐
☐
☐
☐
☐

- [ ]
- [ ]
- [ ]
- [ ]
- [ ]
- [ ]
- [ ]
- [ ]
- [ ]
- [ ]
- [ ]
- [ ]
- [ ]
- [ ]
- [ ]
- [ ]
- [ ]

ACCOUNTABILITY/ PARTNER	SCHEDULE	DAY	TIME

GOALS

I CAN DO THIS

I AM GOING TO

ACTION/PLAN

ACTION STEPS & MILESTONES
☐
☐
☐
☐
☐
☐
☐
☐
☐
☐
☐
☐
☐
☐

- [ ]
- [ ]
- [ ]
- [ ]
- [ ]
- [ ]
- [ ]
- [ ]
- [ ]
- [ ]
- [ ]
- [ ]
- [ ]
- [ ]
- [ ]
- [ ]
- [ ]

ACCOUNTABILITY/ PARTNER	SCHEDULE	DAY	TIME

GOALS

I CAN DO THIS

I AM GOING TO

ACTION/PLAN

ACTION STEPS & MILESTONES
☐
☐
☐
☐
☐
☐
☐
☐
☐
☐
☐
☐
☐
☐

☐
☐
☐
☐
☐
☐
☐
☐
☐
☐
☐
☐
☐
☐
☐
☐
☐

ACCOUNTABILITY/ PARTNER	SCHEDULE	DAY	TIME

GOALS

I CAN DO THIS

I AM GOING TO

ACTION/PLAN

ACTION STEPS & MILESTONES
☐
☐
☐
☐
☐
☐
☐
☐
☐
☐
☐
☐
☐
☐

- [ ]
- [ ]
- [ ]
- [ ]
- [ ]
- [ ]
- [ ]
- [ ]
- [ ]
- [ ]
- [ ]
- [ ]
- [ ]
- [ ]
- [ ]
- [ ]
- [ ]

ACCOUNTABILITY/ PARTNER	SCHEDULE	DAY	TIME

GOALS

I CAN DO THIS

I AM GOING TO

ACTION/PLAN

ACTION STEPS & MILESTONES
☐
☐
☐
☐
☐
☐
☐
☐
☐
☐
☐
☐
☐
☐

- [ ]
- [ ]
- [ ]
- [ ]
- [ ]
- [ ]
- [ ]
- [ ]
- [ ]
- [ ]
- [ ]
- [ ]
- [ ]
- [ ]
- [ ]
- [ ]
- [ ]

ACCOUNTABILITY/ PARTNER	SCHEDULE	DAY	TIME

GOALS

I CAN DO THIS

I AM GOING TO

ACTION/PLAN

ACTION STEPS & MILESTONES
☐
☐
☐
☐
☐
☐
☐
☐
☐
☐
☐
☐
☐
☐

ACCOUNTABILITY/ PARTNER	SCHEDULE	DAY	TIME

GOALS

I CAN DO THIS

I AM GOING TO

ACTION/PLAN

ACTION STEPS & MILESTONES
☐
☐
☐
☐
☐
☐
☐
☐
☐
☐
☐
☐
☐
☐

- [ ]
- [ ]
- [ ]
- [ ]
- [ ]
- [ ]
- [ ]
- [ ]
- [ ]
- [ ]
- [ ]
- [ ]
- [ ]
- [ ]
- [ ]
- [ ]
- [ ]

ACCOUNTABILITY/ PARTNER	SCHEDULE	DAY	TIME

GOALS

I CAN DO THIS

I AM GOING TO

ACTION/PLAN

ACTION STEPS & MILESTONES
☐
☐
☐
☐
☐
☐
☐
☐
☐
☐
☐
☐
☐
☐

- [ ]
- [ ]
- [ ]
- [ ]
- [ ]
- [ ]
- [ ]
- [ ]
- [ ]
- [ ]
- [ ]
- [ ]
- [ ]
- [ ]
- [ ]
- [ ]
- [ ]

ACCOUNTABILITY/ PARTNER	SCHEDULE	DAY	TIME

GOALS

I CAN DO THIS

I AM GOING TO

ACTION/PLAN

ACTION STEPS & MILESTONES
☐
☐
☐
☐
☐
☐
☐
☐
☐
☐
☐
☐
☐
☐

☐
☐
☐
☐
☐
☐
☐
☐
☐
☐
☐
☐
☐
☐
☐
☐
☐

ACCOUNTABILITY/ PARTNER	SCHEDULE	DAY	TIME

GOALS

I CAN DO THIS

I AM GOING TO

ACTION/PLAN

ACTION STEPS & MILESTONES
☐
☐
☐
☐
☐
☐
☐
☐
☐
☐
☐
☐
☐
☐

ACCOUNTABILITY/ PARTNER	SCHEDULE	DAY	TIME

GOALS

I CAN DO THIS

I AM GOING TO

ACTION/PLAN

ACTION STEPS & MILESTONES
☐
☐
☐
☐
☐
☐
☐
☐
☐
☐
☐
☐
☐
☐

- [ ]
- [ ]
- [ ]
- [ ]
- [ ]
- [ ]
- [ ]
- [ ]
- [ ]
- [ ]
- [ ]
- [ ]
- [ ]
- [ ]
- [ ]
- [ ]
- [ ]

ACCOUNTABILITY/ PARTNER	SCHEDULE	DAY	TIME

GOALS

I CAN DO THIS

I AM GOING TO

ACTION/PLAN

ACTION STEPS & MILESTONES
☐
☐
☐
☐
☐
☐
☐
☐
☐
☐
☐
☐
☐
☐

☐
☐
☐
☐
☐
☐
☐
☐
☐
☐
☐
☐
☐
☐
☐
☐
☐

ACCOUNTABILITY/ PARTNER	SCHEDULE	DAY	TIME

GOALS

I CAN DO THIS

I AM GOING TO

ACTION/PLAN

ACTION STEPS & MILESTONES
☐
☐
☐
☐
☐
☐
☐
☐
☐
☐
☐
☐
☐
☐

- [ ]
- [ ]
- [ ]
- [ ]
- [ ]
- [ ]
- [ ]
- [ ]
- [ ]
- [ ]
- [ ]
- [ ]
- [ ]
- [ ]
- [ ]
- [ ]
- [ ]

ACCOUNTABILITY/ PARTNER	SCHEDULE	DAY	TIME

GOALS

I CAN DO THIS

I AM GOING TO

ACTION/PLAN

ACTION STEPS & MILESTONES
☐
☐
☐
☐
☐
☐
☐
☐
☐
☐
☐
☐
☐
☐

ACCOUNTABILITY/ PARTNER	SCHEDULE	DAY	TIME

GOALS

I CAN DO THIS

I AM GOING TO

ACTION/PLAN

ACTION STEPS & MILESTONES
☐
☐
☐
☐
☐
☐
☐
☐
☐
☐
☐
☐
☐
☐

- [ ]
- [ ]
- [ ]
- [ ]
- [ ]
- [ ]
- [ ]
- [ ]
- [ ]
- [ ]
- [ ]
- [ ]
- [ ]
- [ ]
- [ ]
- [ ]
- [ ]

ACCOUNTABILITY/ PARTNER	SCHEDULE	DAY	TIME

GOALS

I CAN DO THIS

I AM GOING TO

ACTION/PLAN

ACTION STEPS & MILESTONES
☐
☐
☐
☐
☐
☐
☐
☐
☐
☐
☐
☐
☐
☐

- [ ]
- [ ]
- [ ]
- [ ]
- [ ]
- [ ]
- [ ]
- [ ]
- [ ]
- [ ]
- [ ]
- [ ]
- [ ]
- [ ]
- [ ]
- [ ]
- [ ]

ACCOUNTABILITY/ PARTNER	SCHEDULE	DAY	TIME

GOALS

I CAN DO THIS

I AM GOING TO

ACTION/PLAN

ACTION STEPS & MILESTONES
☐
☐
☐
☐
☐
☐
☐
☐
☐
☐
☐
☐
☐
☐

- [ ]
- [ ]
- [ ]
- [ ]
- [ ]
- [ ]
- [ ]
- [ ]
- [ ]
- [ ]
- [ ]
- [ ]
- [ ]
- [ ]
- [ ]
- [ ]
- [ ]

ACCOUNTABILITY/ PARTNER	SCHEDULE	DAY	TIME

GOALS

I CAN DO THIS

I AM GOING TO

ACTION/PLAN

ACTION STEPS & MILESTONES

- [ ]
- [ ]
- [ ]
- [ ]
- [ ]
- [ ]
- [ ]
- [ ]
- [ ]
- [ ]
- [ ]
- [ ]
- [ ]
- [ ]

☐
☐
☐
☐
☐
☐
☐
☐
☐
☐
☐
☐
☐
☐
☐
☐
☐

ACCOUNTABILITY/ PARTNER	SCHEDULE	DAY	TIME

GOALS

I CAN DO THIS

I AM GOING TO

ACTION/PLAN

ACTION STEPS & MILESTONES
☐
☐
☐
☐
☐
☐
☐
☐
☐
☐
☐
☐
☐
☐

- [ ]
- [ ]
- [ ]
- [ ]
- [ ]
- [ ]
- [ ]
- [ ]
- [ ]
- [ ]
- [ ]
- [ ]
- [ ]
- [ ]
- [ ]
- [ ]
- [ ]

ACCOUNTABILITY/ PARTNER	SCHEDULE	DAY	TIME

GOALS

I CAN DO THIS

I AM GOING TO

ACTION/PLAN

ACTION STEPS & MILESTONES
☐
☐
☐
☐
☐
☐
☐
☐
☐
☐
☐
☐
☐
☐

☐
☐
☐
☐
☐
☐
☐
☐
☐
☐
☐
☐
☐
☐
☐
☐
☐

ACCOUNTABILITY/ PARTNER	SCHEDULE	DAY	TIME

87883238R00083

Made in the USA
Columbia, SC
21 January 2018